Facts About the Donkey

By Lisa Strattin

© 2019 Lisa Strattin

Facts for Kids Picture Books by Lisa Strattin

Harlequin Macaw, Vol 34

Downy Woodpecker, Vol 37

Frilled Lizard, Vol 39

Purple Finch, Vol 48

Poison Dart Frogs, Vol 50

Giant Otter, Vol 57

Hornbill, Vol 67

Dwarf Lemur, Vol 73

Giant Squirrel, Vol 76

Star Tortoise, Vol 79

Sign Up for New Release Emails Here

http://LisaStrattin.com/subscribe-here

Monthly Surprise Box

http://KidCraftsByLisa.com

All rights reserved. No part of this book may be reproduced by any means whatsoever without the written permission from the author, except brief portions quoted for purpose of review.

All information in this book has been carefully researched and checked for factual accuracy. However, the author and publisher makes no warranty, express or implied, that the information contained herein is appropriate for every individual, situation or purpose and assume no responsibility for errors or omissions. The reader assumes the risk and full responsibility for all actions, and the author will not be held responsible for any loss or damage, whether consequential, incidental, special or otherwise, that may result from the information presented in this book.

All images are free for use or purchased from stock photo sites for commercial use.

Some coloring pages might be of the general species due to lack of available images.

I have relied on my own observations as well as many different sources for this book and I have done my best to check facts and give credit where it is due. In the event that any material is used without proper permission, please contact me so that the oversight can be corrected.

Contents

INTRODUCTION 7

CHARACTERISTICS 9

APPEARANCE 11

LIFE STAGES 13

LIFE SPAN 15

SIZE 17

HABITAT 19

DIET 21

FRIENDS AND ENEMIES 23

SUITABILITY AS PETS 25

PLUSH DONKEY TOY 38

MONTHLY SURPRISE BOX 39

INTRODUCTION

Donkeys were supposedly domesticated around 5,000 years ago in the north east of Africa. The domestication if donkeys soon spread across the globe, with people mainly using the donkeys to help carry heavy loads and transport goods long distances.

CHARACTERISTICS

There are thought to be more than 44 million donkeys throughout the world, with around 11 million of them found in China. Scientists believe that the real number of donkeys could be much higher than this as many donkeys are not counted by anyone.

They are said to have a relatively stubborn temperament, but once the owner of the donkey has become a friend, the donkey is extremely loyal and hard-working. Their self-preservation instincts are strong. They will refuse to move forward, no matter how hard you pull at the lead, if they sense danger or if they are overburdened. They pass this valuable trait on to the mule.

Donkeys are also thought to have a calming effect over distressed horses and are often put into fields with horses as they make great companions for them.

APPEARANCE

Despite the obvious similarities between a donkey and a horse, the offspring of a donkey and a horse mating, which is called a mule, will always be infertile, due to a genetic malfunction that occurs when two different species mate. So mules cannot mate and have babies at all. This is also the case when other different species of them interbreed, such as the onager and the Somali wild ass.

LIFE STAGES

Once a male donkey becomes about two years of age it will mate with another donkey. A female donkey is called a jennet and she will be pregnant for 12 months at which time her baby, called a foal, is born.

LIFE SPAN

Normally, a donkey will live to between 15-30 years. However, some have been known to live as long as 40 years old.

SIZE

Donkeys grow 35 to 51 inches tall at the shoulder and weigh between 400 and 600 pounds as adults!

HABITAT

Wild donkeys have adapted to living in desert environments and because of this, they have very hardy immune and digestive systems. This allows the donkey to be able to process and gain nutrition from vegetation, like weeds. that many other species of animal have great difficulty gaining any nutrition when they might eat this.

DIET

Donkeys are herbivores. They eat mostly gasses, and vegetables. They will even eat weeds if they are growing in their habitat!

FRIENDS AND ENEMIES

Donkeys are friends with horses, one another and can be domesticated to become great friends with people as well. They are a help to people in carrying burdens on their backs in many agricultural and desert environments.

Predators of the donkey include foxes, wolves and lions. These animals will hunt and kill donkeys in the wild.

SUITABILITY AS PETS

A donkey can be domesticated easily. Although they are stubborn, they are great to have as a tame animal if you have enough land where they can graze and roam around freely.

It's certainly not a pet you want to bring into the house, but you can have one that will allow you to come close and pet it, just like a tame horse.

COLOR ME

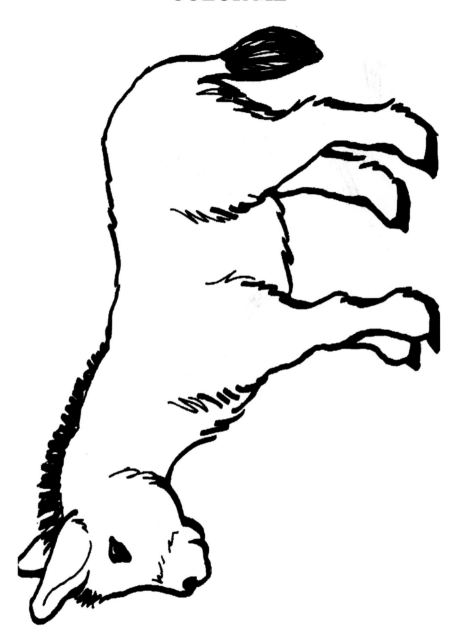

COLOR ME

COLOR ME

COLOR ME

COLOR ME

COLOR ME

COLOR ME

COLOR ME

COLOR ME

COLOR ME

Please leave me a review here:

http://lisastrattin.com/Review-Vol-179

For more Kindle Downloads Visit Lisa Strattin Author Page on Amazon Author Central

http://amazon.com/author/lisastrattin

To see upcoming titles, visit my website at LisaStrattin.com– all books available on kindle!

http://lisastrattin.com

PLUSH DONKEY TOY

You can get one by copying and pasting this link into your browser:

http://lisastrattin.com/PlushDonkey

MONTHLY SURPRISE BOX

Get yours by copying and pasting this link into your browser

http://KidCraftsByLisa.com

Made in the USA
Columbia, SC
03 December 2021